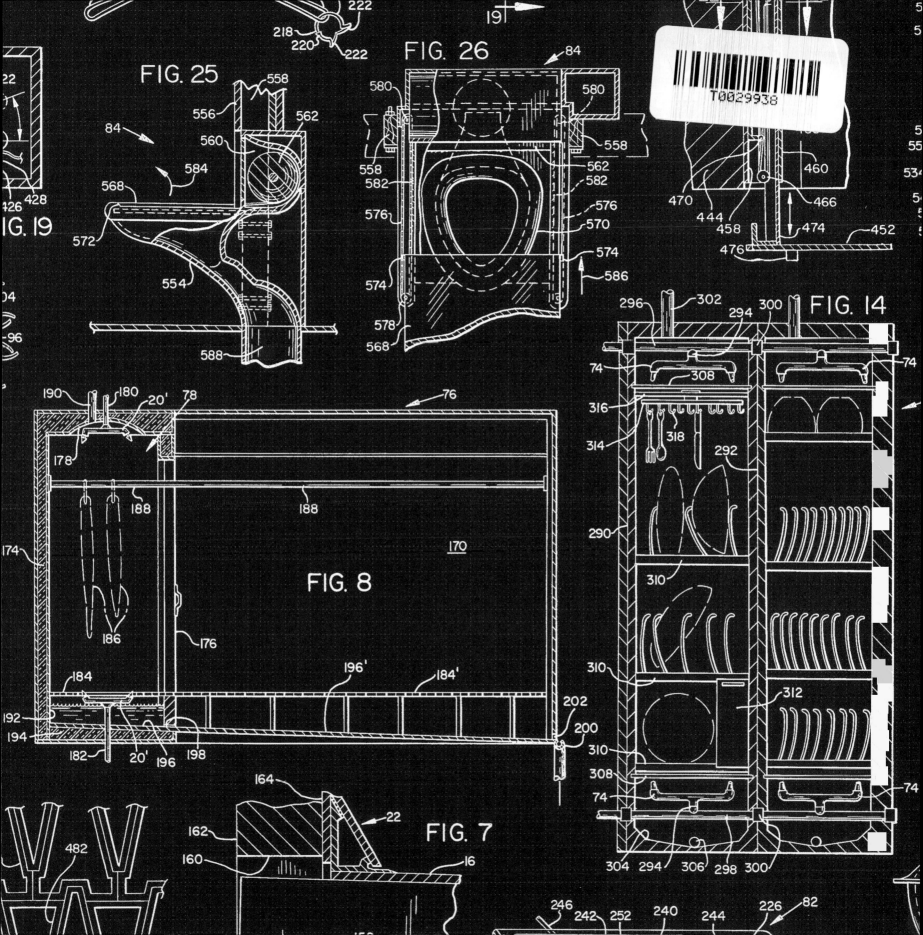

To Rosie, my most enthusiastic reader — L. D.

To H. and H., with love — S. R.

For Rory and Ewan — M. R.

THE HOUSE

THAT CLEANED ITSELF:

THE TRUE STORY OF FRANCES GABE'S
(MOSTLY) MARVELOUS INVENTION

BY **LAURA DERSHEWITZ**
AND **SUSAN ROMBERG**
ILLUSTRATED BY **MEGHANN RADER**

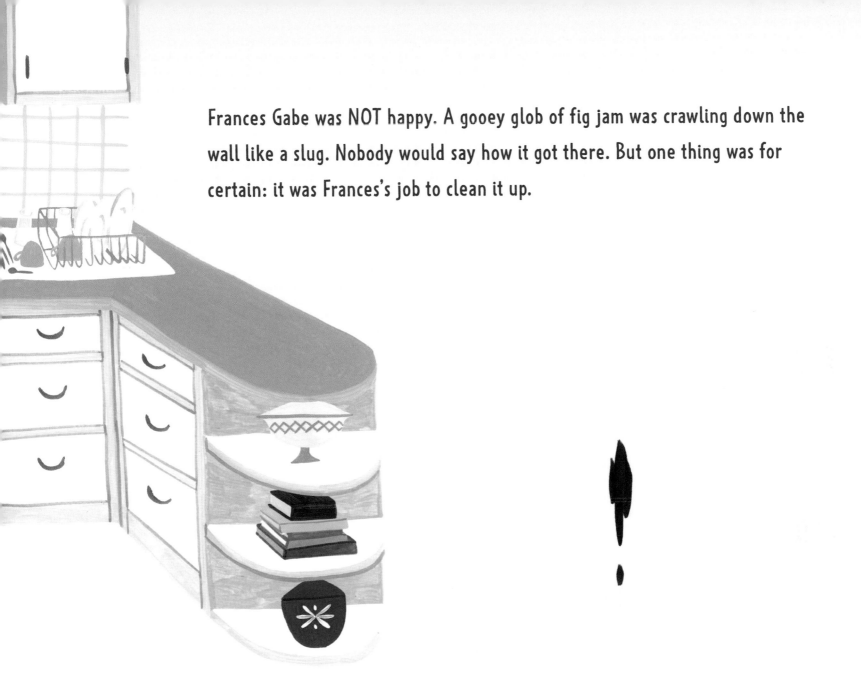

Frances Gabe was NOT happy. A gooey glob of fig jam was crawling down the wall like a slug. Nobody would say how it got there. But one thing was for certain: it was Frances's job to clean it up.

After all, it was long ago, when women were expected to do all the scrubbing

and wiping

and rinsing.

But Frances couldn't stand back-breaking, knee-creaking housework. She found cleaning "a nerve-twangling bore."

Now some people in this sticky situation might have just grabbed a rag and started to scrub. But not Frances. Oh no, not Frances! Sick of scrubbing, she did something about it.

With her "jaw set hard," Frances marched outside for the garden hose, dragged it into the kitchen, aimed it at the wall, and fired.

All Frances had to do was stand there. The wall practically cleaned itself! And that day, as the story goes, she had the beginnings of an idea.

"I picked up a pencil and began scribbling. I thought I was just doodling.

Then I stopped and looked, and there was the self-cleaning house."

Now there's a funny thing about ideas. Sometimes a good one will sit for a long time. Eventually it'll grow pesky and gnaw at you till you take notice.

And so it was for Frances. Years passed, daily chores dragged on, and her children grew up and moved away. As her life became quieter, her old idea became louder. *Water under pressure cleaned the wall, but could it clean more?* she wondered. *What about the rest of the walls, the floors, the appliances, and the furniture? What if it could all clean itself?*

It was time for Frances to do something about it. No more endless sweeping and mopping and dusting! She would help women everywhere by creating the world's first self-cleaning house.

Frances got right to work testing and tinkering in her studio. She studied the properties of water and experimented with varnishes and resins.

At times Frances had problems making things work. At times people thought she'd never succeed.

"So impractical!" said some.

"Completely foolish!" said others.

Many would have quit. But Frances carried on. "I'm me," she said. "I do things." And so she did, until she completed her house.

And it wasn't just any old house.

Frances's house was unlike any you've ever seen. When everything went as planned, each room cleaned itself at the touch of a button.

All this washing involved a lot of brand new inventions. Now if some people had thought up even one or two of them, they might feel pretty proud of themselves, as well they should. But Frances cooked up close to seventy!

So how exactly did Frances's house work?

Picture an automatic carwash, with soap suds flying all over the place. Now picture that carwash in each room of a house!

Frances installed sprinklers in the ceilings to spray soapy water for washing and clean water for rinsing. Then air jets were supposed to dry the place off.

"Water's like electricity. It will take the easiest path, whether it spoils things or not. It doesn't give a darn.

But I whipped it. Now the water does just what I want."

But try as it might, the hot air couldn't dry up the puddles. So Frances did something about it. She slanted the floors to guide the water outside through a system of drains.

One drain even emptied into her Great Dane's doghouse, sometimes surprising the old girl with a bath!

The sprinklers took care of the walls and floors, but some rooms needed extra attention. In the bathroom, Frances built pumps to splash more water around the tub and sink. She even made special air jets that could dry the bathtub—and the bather!

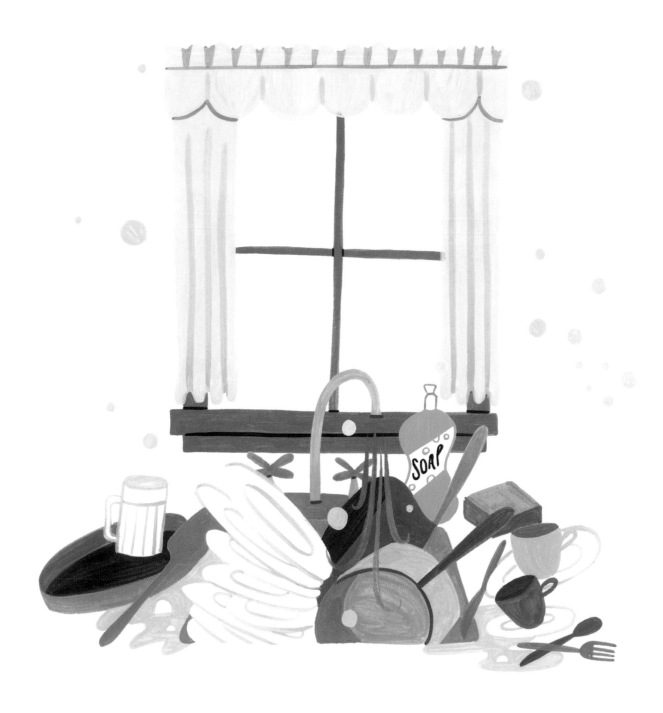

In the kitchen, Frances tackled the tiresome job of loading and unloading the dishwasher.

She designed a dish cupboard that washed
and stored the dishes in the same place.

To take the labor out of laundry, Frances invented a waterproof cabinet called a "clothes freshener," where she hung up her dirty shirts and pants and let a mini-sprinkler system do the rest.

After the clothes were clean and dry, she guided them to the closet using a pulley system she rigged up herself.

Now you might be wondering about the books and the rugs and everything else in a house that's just not meant to get wet.

Never fear—Frances did something about those too! To protect her books, she made watertight jackets. She created a water-resistant fabric for furniture and built her bed its very own umbrella. Frances didn't fret about rugs and curtains. She simply didn't have any.

When people caught wind of Frances's house, they traveled from far and wide to see it.

Newspapers and TV shows told stories about her.

Museums displayed models of her work.

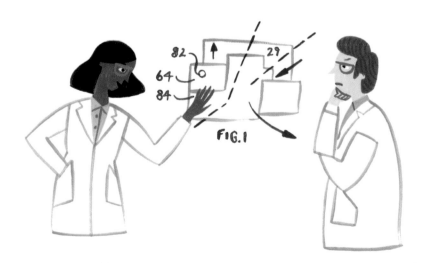

Scientists studied her ideas.

One famous writer even suggested that Frances should appear on Mount Rushmore, along with the presidents!

So what happened to Frances's humdinger of an idea?

Why don't all of us live in self-cleaning houses?

Some thought it would be too unpleasant to walk around in a raincoat at home.

Others thought a home with so many machines would be too troublesome to maintain.

the world over. Ten years ago they told me I was 20 years ahead of my time..."

The world may not have been ready for a self-cleaning house. But it always needs inventors and dreamers and doers, like Frances. It always needs big ideas.

There's another funny thing about ideas, you know. New ones tend
to connect to old ones, like one plumbing pipe joining to the next.
Maybe one day a young inventor will figure out how to build on
Frances's ideas—and go out and do something about it. Maybe that
"something" will be just enough to end household chores for good.

And from that day on, no one will have to clean up fig jam again!

Authors' Note

Frances Grace Arnholtz was born in Idaho in 1915. Shortly after graduating from Girls Polytechnic School in Portland, Oregon, she married Herbert Bateson, and the couple had two children. When her marriage ended in the 1970s, Frances wanted a fresh start. She began by changing her name. Frances borrowed the *G, A,* and *B* from her middle and last names and added an *E* to form *Gabe.* Her new name was one of many things that Frances Gabe invented on her own.

Of course, most of her inventions related to her one-of-a-kind house. Frances's impatience for housework began long before the fig jam incident. It "stuck in my craw even when I was a kid," she said. Frances felt it was particularly unfair that the mindless, endless, physically demanding tasks she described as "back abuse" were reserved for women.

Surely Frances wasn't alone in these thoughts. But she was alone in how she confronted them. Despite having limited funds and no college education, she found a way to build a self-cleaning house. When there was something she didn't know, she figured

it out. For example, she made and tested new resins in her kitchen, and she studied water in a shower stall in her yard. Frances faced criticism—from people who doubted her abilities, neighbors displeased with her uncompromising nature and the cement mixer on her lawn, and even women who feared she was putting them out of a job. Still, Frances persisted.

Frances completed her project in the 1980s. It drew interest and acclaim, at one point even attracting the attention of scientists from NASA. But Frances wanted more. She believed that her invention could offer new freedoms for women and benefit other groups, too. "I want to eliminate all unnecessary motion so that handicapped and elderly people can care for their homes themselves," Frances said. "My system will allow people to do so by pushing a few buttons."

Despite its great promise, the self-cleaning house was ultimately deemed impractical, and Frances's wish never came true. Over time, the house fell into disrepair, and eventually, Frances moved out. When she died in 2016 at age 101, her invention had been all but forgotten.

So why write about Frances Gabe and the self-cleaning house? Frances embodied some of the qualities we admire most: she was a problem-solver, a hard and scrappy worker, and an exceptionally innovative thinker. Moreover, she used her ingenuity to try to improve life for herself and others. Like her invention, Frances was imperfect but a true, sparkling original.

Though the self-cleaning house was not a commercial success, technology tends to evolve, with new ideas building on old ones. Perhaps one day a young scientist or engineer will decide to pick up where Frances left off.

Bibliography

We would like to thank Lily Benson, Allyn Brown, and Patrick Roden for sharing their memories of Frances Gabe. We are also grateful to Debra Hughes of the Hagley Museum and Library for providing photographs of and information about the self-cleaning house.

Bateson, Frances G. Self-cleaning building construction. US Patent 4428085, filed April 21, 1980, and issued January 31, 1984.

Benson, Lily. "A Tour of the Self-Cleaning House." Filmed in 2015. Video, 11:00. http://lilybenson.com/self-cleaning-house.

Brown, Patricia Leigh. "Son of Carwash, the Self-Cleaning House." *New York Times,* January 17, 2002. www.nytimes.com/2002/01/17/garden/son-of-carwash-the-self-cleaning-house.html.

Byrne, Michael. "RIP Frances Gabe, Inventor of the Self-Cleaning House." *Motherboard,* July 19, 2017. https://motherboard.vice.com/en_us/article/9kw87e/rip-frances-gabe-inventor-of-the-self-cleaning-house.

Dolan, Mike. "Mrs. Gabe and Her Self-Cleaning House." *Christian Science Monitor,* May 12, 1982. www.csmonitor.com/1982/0512/051235.html.

Faircloth, Kelly. "RIP This Inventor of a Self-Cleaning House." *Jezebel,* July 19, 2017. https://pictorial.jezebel.com/rip-this-inventor-of-a-self-cleaning-house-1797055973.

Fox, Margalit. "Frances Gabe, Creator of the Only Self-Cleaning Home, Dies at 101." *New York Times,* July 18, 2017. www.nytimes.com/2017/07/18/us/frances-gabe-dead-inventor-of-self-cleaning-house.html.

"Frances Gabe's Self-Cleaning House." Reported by Carl Click, recorded by Milt Ritter, *KGW8 News,* January 17, 1990. Video, 2:09. http://www.kgw.com/video/news/special-reports/archive-video/archive-frances-gabes-self-cleaning-house/283-2666270.

Hughes, Debra. "Frances Gabe and Her Amazing Self-Cleaning House!" Hagley Museum and Library, October 23, 2017. www.hagley.org/librarynews/frances-gabe-and-her-amazing-self-cleaning-house.

Johnson, John. "She Invented a Self-Cleaning House, but World Wasn't Ready." *Newser,* July 19, 2017. www.newser.com/story/245915/she-invented-a-self-cleaning-house-decades-ago.html.

Kennedy, Pagan. "Geniuses, Mad Scientists, and Inventors." *Dwell,* February 2001, 70–71.

Korfhage, Matthew. "Capture or Asylum: Chuck Palahniuk's *Fugitives and Refugees* 10 Years Later." *Willamette Week,* July 2, 2013. www.wweek.com/portland/article-20859-capture-or-asylum.html.

Lemelson-MIT. "Frances Gabe: The Self-Cleaning House." https://lemelson.mit.edu/resources/frances-gabe.

McMurran, Kristin. "Frances Gabe's Self-Cleaning House Could Mean New Rights of Spring for Housewives." *People,* March 29, 1982. http://people.com/archive/frances-gabes-self-cleaning-house-could-mean-new-rights-of-spring-for-housewives-vol-17-no-12.

Padnani, Amisha. "The House That Did the Housework." *New York Times,* July 18, 2017. www.nytimes.com/2017/07/18/obituaries/the-house-that-did-the-housework.html.

Palahniuk, Chuck. *Fugitives and Refugees: A Walk in Portland, Oregon.* New York: Crown, 2003.

"Remembering Frances Gabe, Oregon Inventor of the Self-Cleaning House." *Think Out Loud,* reported by Dave Miller, Oregon Public Broadcasting, July 21, 2017. www.opb.org/radio/programs/thinkoutloud/segment/self-cleaning-house-frances-gabe-inventor-oregon/.

Walker, Alissa. "Everything You Need to Read About Frances Gabe, Self-Cleaning House Inventor." *Curbed,* July 21, 2017. www.curbed.com/2017/7/21/16008194/frances-gabe-self-cleaning-house-obituary.

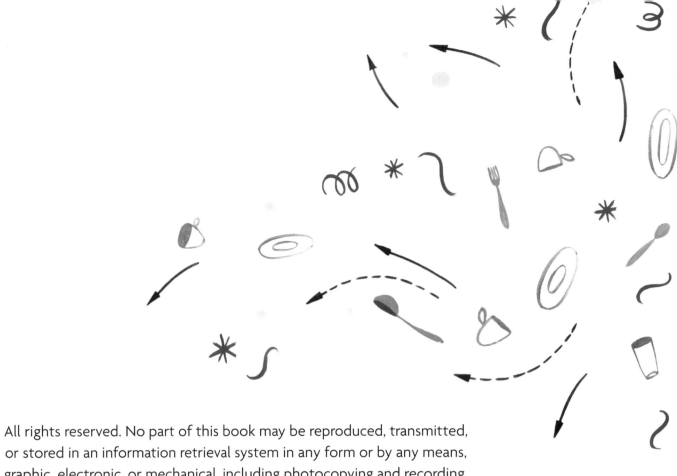

Library of Congress Control Number: 2019900122
ISBN 9781943147656

Text copyright © 2019 by Laura Dershewitz and Susan Romberg
Illustrations copyright © 2019 by Meghann Rader

Published by The Innovation Press
1001 4th Avenue, Suite 3200, Seattle, WA 98154
www.theinnovationpress.com

Printed and bound by Worzalla
Production date June 2019

Cover lettering by Nicole LaRue
Cover art by Meghann Rader
Book layout by Tim Martyn

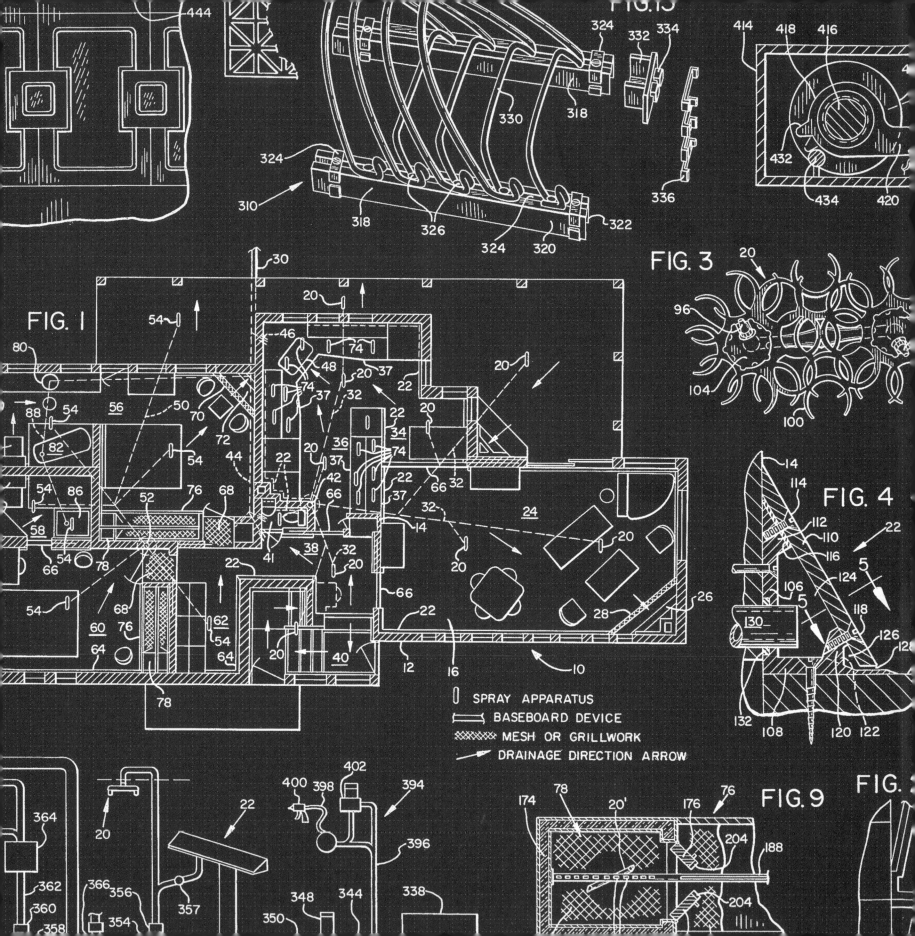

FIG. 13

444

330

318

324 332 334

318

336

414 418 416

432

434 420

310

324

318 326 324 320 322

FIG. 1

FIG. 3

20

80

30

54

20

20

96

104

100

88 54

56

50

70

46

74

48 20 37

74 37 32

22

20

34

20

66 32

FIG. 4

14

114

82

72

54

44

22

20

36

74

22

37

42

66

32

22

20

24

112

110

116

106

124

5

5

118

126

58

54 86

66 54 78

52

76

68

41

38

66

32

32

20

20

20

14

66

26

28

130

132

108 120 122

54

60 76

62

54

64

22

20

40

20

22

16

12

10

SPRAY APPARATUS

BASEBOARD DEVICE

MESH OR GRILLWORK

DRAINAGE DIRECTION ARROW

78

364

362

360

358

366 356

357

354

20

22

400 398 402

394

396

338

348 344

350

FIG. 9

FIG.

174

78

20'

176

76

204

188

204